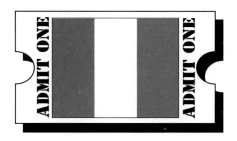

Leaning Tower
Of Pisa

FACES
AND
PLACES

# ITALY

BY MARY BERENDES

THE CHILD'S WORLD®, INC.

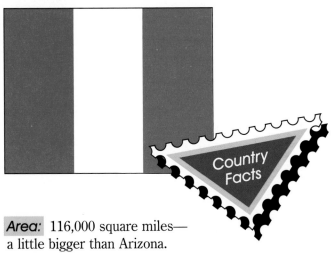

**Country Facts**

*Area:* 116,000 square miles— a little bigger than Arizona.

*Population:* About 59 million people.

*Capital City:* Rome.

*Other Important Cities:* Milan, Naples, Turin, Florence, Venice.

*Money:* The lira.

*National Language:* Italian.

*National Song:* "Inno di Mameli," or "Mameli's Hymn." Some people also call the song "Fratelli d'Italia," or "Brothers of Italy."

*National Holiday:* Constitution Day on June 2.

*National Flag:* Three vertical stripes of green, white, and red.

*Heads of Government:* The president of Italy and the prime minister of Italy.

Text copyright © 1999 by The Child's World®, Inc. All rights reserved. No part of this book may be reproduced or utilized in any form or by any means without written permission from the publisher. Printed in the United States of America.

Library of Congress Cataloging-in-Publication Data
Berendes, Mary
Italy / by Mary Berendes.
Series: "Faces and Places".
p. cm.
Includes index.
Summary: Describes the geography, history, people, and customs of Italy.
ISBN 1-56766-581-0 (library : reinforced : alk. paper)

1. Italy — Juvenile literature.
[1. Italy.] I. Title.

DG417.B47 1999
945 — dc21

98-43003
CIP
AC

**GRAPHIC DESIGN**
Robert A. Honey, Seattle

**PHOTO RESEARCH**
James R. Rothaus / James R. Rothaus & Associates

**ELECTRONIC PRE–PRESS PRODUCTION**
Robert E. Bonaker / Graphic Design & Consulting Co.

**PHOTOGRAPHY**
Cover photo: Sicilian Boys in Elementary School by Jonathan Blair/Corbis

Table
of
Contents

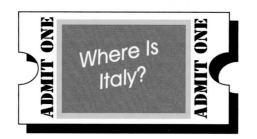

From far away, Earth is a colorful place. Blues, reds, browns, greens, and whites can all be seen. The huge blue areas are Earth's oceans. The white wisps are clouds. The big brown patches are land areas called **continents**. Some continents are made up of many different countries.

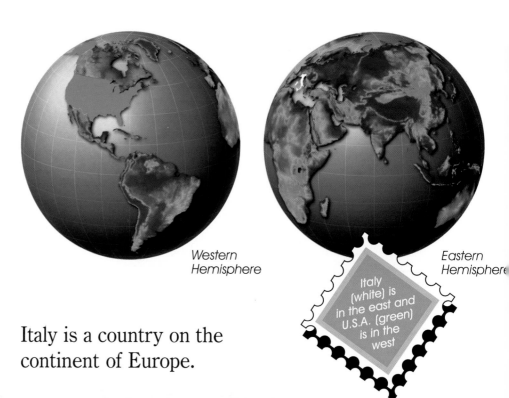

Western Hemisphere

Eastern Hemisphere

Italy (white) is in the east and U.S.A. (green) is in the west

Italy is a country on the continent of Europe.

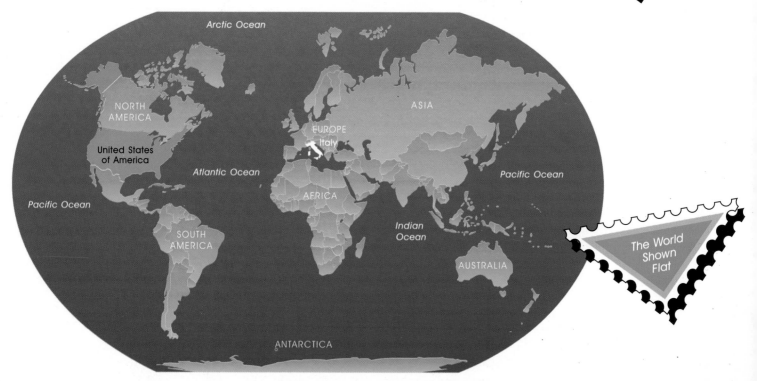

Arctic Ocean

NORTH AMERICA

United States of America

Atlantic Ocean

Pacific Ocean

SOUTH AMERICA

ASIA

EUROPE
Italy

AFRICA

Indian Ocean

Pacific Ocean

AUSTRALIA

ANTARCTICA

The World Shown Flat

GERMANY

AUSTRIA

FRANCE

HUNGARY

SWITZERLAND

SLOVENIA

CROATIA

BOSNIA
AND
HERZEGOVINA

YUGOSLAVIA

*Adriatic Sea*

ITALY

CORSICA

ALBANIA

SARDINIA

GREECE

*Mediterranean
Sea*

SICILY

*Mediterranean
Sea*

ALGERIA

TUNISIA

Close-Up
of
Italy

Hills Slope
Down To
Beach At
Positano

South Tyrol
Alps
Dolomites

ITALIAN PENINSULA

Apennines

SARDINIA

Positano

SICILY

Mount Etna

Michael S. Yamashita/Corbis

Italy is a **peninsula**. That means it is a piece of land that is surrounded by water on almost all sides. On the Italian peninsula, there are many different types of land. There are thick, green forests and flat, grassy plains. There are sandy beaches, deep valleys, and steep cliffs. There are also beautiful mountains in Italy. The snowy *Alps* are in the north. Father south, the *Apennines* can be found.

River Of Lava Flows From The Volcano Of Mount Etna

Vittoriano Rastelli/Corbis

Green Fields In Italy's South Tyrol

Galen Rowell/Corbis

Valley In The Dolomites, Italian Alps

Galen Rowell/Corbis

Grapes In
Tuscany
Region

Since there are so many land types in Italy, many kinds of plants can be found. Oak and evergreen trees live in the thick forests of the Alps. Short bushes and grasses grow in lower areas. Italy's warm weather helps olive and grape plants grow in many places, too.

Many kinds of animals make their homes in Italy. Bears, foxes, and wolves all live in the green forests. Wild pigs and deer can be found there, too. In the seas near Italy's shores, fish such as sardines and tuna swim and feed.

Vince Streano/Corbis

Olive Grove
In Puglia
Region

Gray Wolf
In Meadow
Near
Toscana

Marcello Calandrini/Corbis

Vince Streano/Corbis

Alps

■ *Toscana (Tuscany Region)*
● *Monte Amiata*

*Puglia Region* ■

Maurizio Lanini/Corbis

Male Elk
From
Monte Amiata

Hannibal From Africa Crossed The Alps To Attack The Romans

Alps

Latium Region

Rome ☆

Pompeii · Mount Vesuvius
Salerno

Gianni Dagli Orti/Corbis

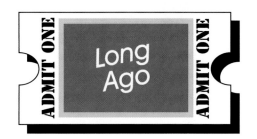

Long Ago

**P**eople have been living in Italy for thousands of years. As towns and cities grew, kingdoms formed. The city of Rome became a very powerful kingdom. The Roman kings, or **emperors**, controlled many other countries and areas for hundreds of years.

David Lees/©Corbis

Paestum Is An Ancient Greek Ruin Near Salerno

As time went by, other countries wanted the power that Italy had. Slowly, different groups came to Italy and fought over the land. The Roman emperors lost their power and other countries took turns ruling. Spain, Germany, France, and Austria all fought over Italy for hundreds of years.

Latium Region, Etruscan Art, From 550-520 BC

Roger Ressmeyer/©Corbis

Pompeii Was Totally Destroyed By Mount Vesuvius (Horizon) In 79 A.D.

Gianni Dagli Orti/Corbis

After years of fighting—even with each other—Italy is peaceful. It has its own government that makes laws to keep people safe. Like many other countries, Italy's people and government sometimes have problems agreeing on ideas. Even so, Italians are working together to make their country strong.

Browsing An Alghero Newsstand To Keep Informed

Kevin Schafer/Corbis

Ornate Interior Of Italian Parliament, Rome

Nicolas Sapieha; Kea Publishing Service Ltd./Corbis

The Press Surrounds A Man From Parliament

Vittoriano Rastelli/Corbis

Dennis Marsico/©Corbis

People Gathered
In Square
In Rome

Families
Enjoy The
Hot Springs
In Saturnia

• San Gimignano
• Saturnia
☆ Rome

Salemi •
*SICILY*

Owen Franken/Corbis

# The People

ADMIT ONE · ADMIT ONE

**I**talians are happy people who like to have fun. They also like to work hard at their jobs. Pride in their country—and in their neighborhoods— is very important to many Italians. Italians show lots of respect and love to their families and friends. In Italy, loved ones are very important.

A Salemi Family Gathers To Harvest Grapes

Jonathan Blair/Corbis

Friends Relax On The Spanish Steps In Rome

Couple Embracing On Street In San Gimignano

Kelly-Mooney Photography/Corbis

Vince Streano/Corbis

17

Richard Glover/Corbis

More than half of Italy's people live in cities and towns. In big cities, there are tall buildings and busy streets. There are markets and restaurants. There are also train stations. In smaller towns, there are churches and small shops. In both cities and towns, most Italians live in apartments.

Life in Italy's countryside is different. People there live in tiny, simple towns. There are no tall buildings or noisy streets. Instead, only short buildings and narrow roads can be found. Rather than drive cars, most country people walk from place to place.

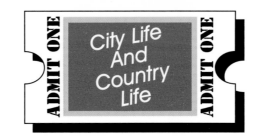
Housing In The Small Town Of San Gimignano

Apartments In Florence Are Close Together

Sandro Vannini/Corbis

Cone Shaped Roofs Of The Puglia Region

Michael Lewis/Corbis

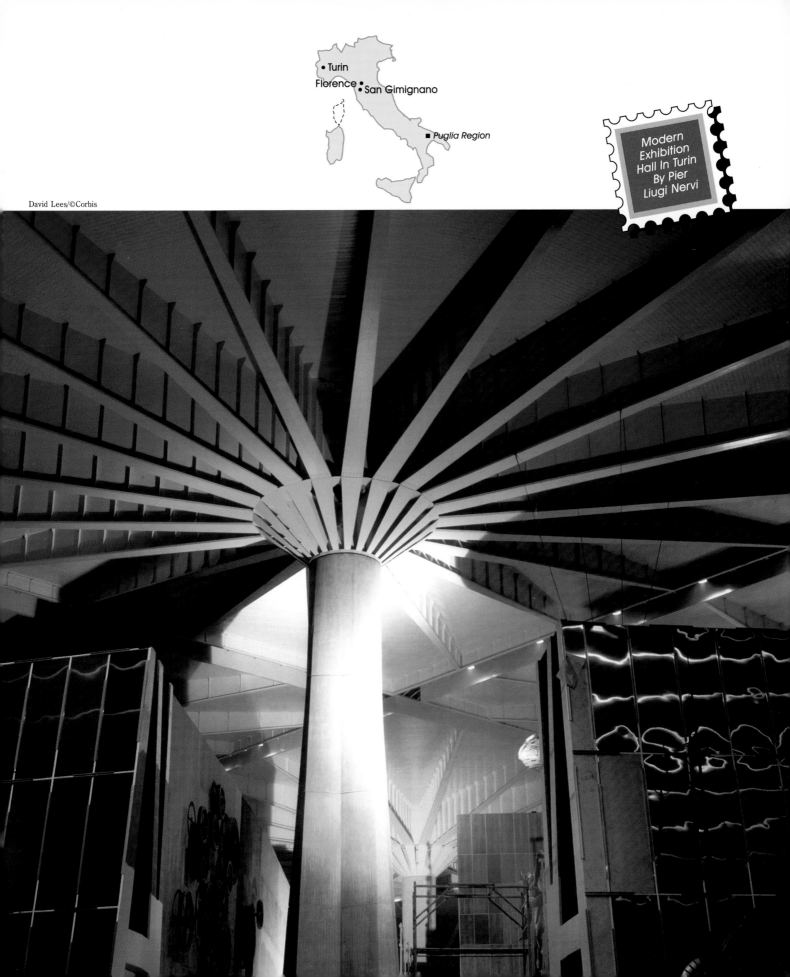

David Lees/©Corbis

• Turin

Florence • San Gimignano

■ Puglia Region

Modern
Exhibition
Hall In Turin
By Pier
Liugi Nervi

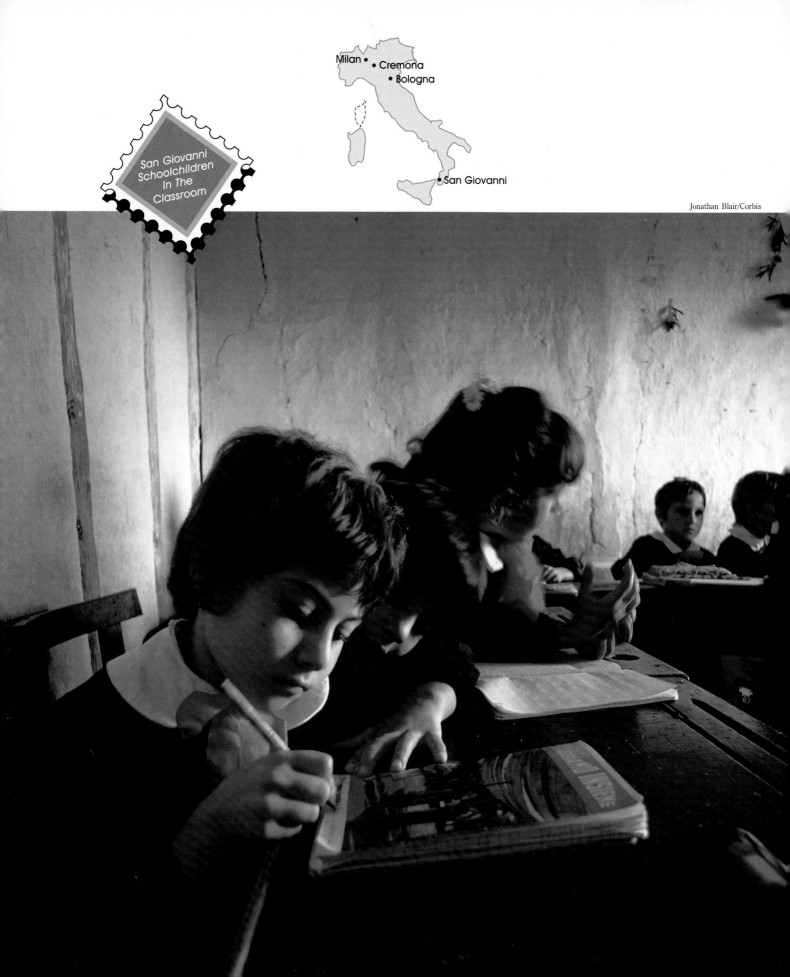

San Giovanni
Schoolchildren
In The
Classroom

Milan • • Cremona
• Bologna

• San Giovanni

Jonathan Blair/Corbis

# Schools And Language

ADMIT ONE · ADMIT ONE

Italian children begin school when they are about six years old. They learn reading, writing, math, and science, just as you do. Many students have art or music classes, too. When they are a little older, Italian children also learn another language, such as English or French.

David Lees/©Corbis

Student Making A Violin In Cremona

Italy's official language is Italian. It is based on an old language called *Latin*. Latin is a beautiful language. It is part of many languages today— even English! In some areas of Italy, people speak a form of Italian called a **dialect**. Each dialect has its own special words and sounds.

Ted Spiegel/Corbis

Girls On A Field Trip To Milan Castle

Student And Professor At University Of Bologna

Jonathan Blair/Corbis

ADMIT ONE ADMIT ONE

Italy is a busy place, and there are many jobs to do. Some people work for big companies such as banks or airlines. Others work in restaurants, shops, hotels, or factories. Many other Italians work on farms raising crops or animals.

Tourism is also an important job in Italy. Tourism is a job where Italians show people from other places about their country. Every year, more and more people are coming to Italy. They want to see and learn about Italy's cities, people, and beautiful land.

Quarrying Treasured Carrara Marble

Hans Georg Roth/Corbis

Tuscany Region Farmhouse On Hill Beside Vineyards

Michael Boys/©Corbis

Family Waits Out Rain To Work In Field In Sicily

Jonathan Blair/Corbis

Venice

Carrara

■ Tuscany Region

SICILY

Bob Krist/Corbis

Gondoliers
Take Passengers
For Rides
In Venice

A Chef
From Alba
Smells A Truffle
Before
Buying

• Alba    • Bologna

Sorrento •

Palermo

*SICILY*

Vittoriano Rastelli/Corbis

Food

Italians love to cook and eat. In fact, Italians are known all over the world for their delicious dishes! **Pasta** is a favorite meal for many people. It is a thin dough that can be shaped in many different ways. Then it is cooked by boiling it in water. When the pasta is ready, it is mixed with everything from meats to cheeses to thick tomato sauces.

Dave Bartruff/Corbis

Italians eat other things, too. Bread, meat, fish, fruit, and vegetables are all popular foods. Italians also like to drink wine with their meals. The wine is often made from grapes that were grown in Italy's own fields.

£22000

£6000 £9

Fruit In A Market In Sorrento

A Bologna Waiter Holds Fresh Pasta

1700

Butcher In Palermo

Jonathan Blair/Corbis

Nik Wheeler/Corbis

# Pastimes

Italians are hard workers, but they like to have fun, too. Skiing, fishing, bicycling, and horse riding are all popular pastimes in Italy. By far, the most important sport for Italians is soccer. It is played almost everywhere—from parks and playgrounds to city streets. In fact, soccer is so important to Italians that every big city has its own team!

Sailboats Competing Near Porto Cervo

Vittoriano Rastelli/Corbis

Boys Playing Soccer In Pisa

Climbers On Mont Blanc In The Alps

Richard Hamilton Smith/Corbis

John Slater/Corbis

Mont Blanc

Alps

Stura di Demonte River

Pisa

Porto Cervo

SARDINIA

Whitewater
Kayaker On
Stura di Demonte
River

Tiziana and Gianni Baldizzone/Corbis

Christmas
Bagpipers
In The Piazza
Navona,
Rome

• Venice

• Assisi
☆ Rome

Trapani •
*SICILY*

David Lees/©Corbis

# Holidays

There are lots of different holidays in Italy. Some holidays are huge celebrations for the whole country. Others are small festivals that are only found in little towns.

Ascension Day Celebraation In Venice

Todd Gipstein/Corbis

May Day Festival In Assisi

Many of the holidays that are celebrated in Italy can also be found in the United States. New Year's Day and Christmas are two of these holidays.

Italy is a beautiful country with proud people. With such pretty land, old buildings, and great food, it is sure to be a place you will want to visit!

Easter Festival In Trapani

Sandro Vannini/Corbis

Daniel Lainé/Corbis

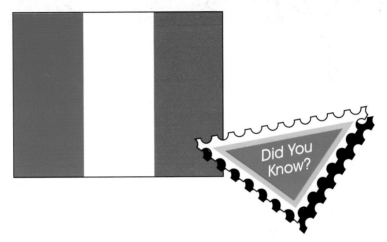

Italy is really called the "Italian Republic." People just say "Italy" for short.

Venice is a very famous Italian city. It was built hundreds of years ago on islands in a lagoon. The water from the sea comes right up to the doorways of many buildings. Instead of using roads and cars, the people of Venice must use boats and bridges to get from place to place.

Italy has two major islands, called Sicily and Sardinia. Sicily has mountains, plains, and a volcano called "Mount Etna." Sardinia is covered mostly by hills and mountains.

Spending time with family and friends is very important to Italians. In fact, many people enjoy a passeggiata (pah–say–jee–YAH–tah) in the evenings. The passeggiata is a slow walk with loved ones. Families and friends talk and laugh as they walk along the streets and parks.

**How Do You Say?**

|  | ITALIAN | HOW TO SAY IT |
| --- | --- | --- |
| Hello | ciao | (CHOW) |
| Goodbye | arrivederci | (ah-ree-vah-DAYR-chee) |
| Please | per favore | (PAYR fah-VOH-RAY) |
| Thank You | grazie | (GRAHTS-yay) |
| One | uno | (OO-no) |
| Two | due | (DOO-ay) |
| Three | tre | (TRAY) |
| Italy | Italia | (ee-TA-lee-yah) |

## Glossary

**continents (KON–tih–nents)**
Most of the land areas on Earth are divided up into huge sections called continents. Italy is on the continent of Europe.

**dialect (DY–uh–lekt)**
A dialect is a different form of a language. In some areas of Italy, dialects of the Italian language can be found.

**emperors (EM–per–rerz)**
An emperor is another name for a king. The city of Rome was ruled by emperors long ago.

**pasta (PAH–stuh)**
Pasta is a thin dough that is shaped in different ways. Pasta is a favorite part of many Italian dishes.

**peninsula (peh–NIN–soo–luh)**
A peninsula is an area of land that has water almost all the way around it. Italy is a peninsula.

**tourism (TOOR–ih–zem)**
The business of showing travelers around a country is called tourism. Tourism is a very important business in Italy.

## Index